A Lume Spento
and Other Early Poems

Ezra Pound in 1909

EZRA POUND

A LUME SPENTO

AND OTHER EARLY POEMS

NEW DIRECTIONS

The photograph reproduced on the binding shows
San Trovaso, Venice; the poet lived in the building
partly hidden by the tree on the right. (Photo
O. Böhm, Venice.)

Library of Congress Catalog Card Number: 65-15670

FIRST PRINTING

COPYRIGHT © 1965 BY EZRA POUND

COPYRIGHT © 1965 BY NEW DIRECTIONS
PUBLISHING CORPORATION

MANUFACTURED IN THE UNITED STATES OF AMERICA

New Directions books are published for James Laughlin
by New Directions Publishing Corporation,
333 Sixth Avenue, New York 14.

CONTENTS

Foreword (1964)

A collection of stale creampuffs. "Chocolate creams, who hath forgotten you?"

At a time when Bill W. was perceiving the "Coroner's Children."

As to why a reprint? No lessons to be learned save the depth of ignorance, or rather the superficiality of non-perception—neither eye nor ear. Ignorance that didn't know the meaning of "Wardour Street."

E.P.

San Ambrogio
19 Ag. '64

A Lume Spento

(1908)

A
LUME
SPENTO

EZRA POUND.

Title page of Pound's first book

This Book was

LA FRAISNE

(THE ASH TREE)

dedicated

*to such as love this same
beauty that I love, somewhat
after mine own fashion.*

But sith one of them has gone out very quickly from
amongst us it is given

A LUME SPENTO

(WITH TAPERS QUENCHED)

in memoriam eius mihi caritate primus

William Brooke Smith

Painter, Dreamer of dreams.

GRACE BEFORE SONG

Lord God of heaven that with mercy dight
    Th' alternate prayer wheel of the night and light
    Eternal hath to thee, and in whose sight
Our days as rain drops in the sea surge fall,

As bright white drops upon a leaden sea
Grant so my songs to this grey folk may be:

As drops that dream and gleam and falling catch the
        sun,
Evan'scent mirrors every opal one
Of such his splendor as their compass is,
So, bold My Songs, seek ye such death as this.

When the soul is exhausted in fire, then doth the spirit return unto its primal nature and there is upon it a peace great and of the woodland

"magna pax et silvestris."

Then becometh it kin to the faun and the dryad, a woodland-dweller amid the rocks and streams

"consociis faunis dryadisque inter saxa sylvarum"

Janus of Basel.*

Also has Mr. Yeats in his *Celtic Twilight* treated of such, and I because in such a mood, feeling myself divided between myself corporal and a self aetherial, "a dweller by streams and in wood-land," eternal because simple in elements

"Aeternus quia simplex naturae."

Being freed of the weight of a soul "capable of salvation or damnation," a grievous striving thing that after much straining was mercifully taken from me; as had one passed saying as one in the Book of the Dead, "I, lo I, am the assembler of souls," and had taken it with him, leaving me thus *simplex naturae,* even so at peace and trans-sentient as a wood pool I made it.

The Legend thus: "Miraut de Garzelas, after the pains he bore a-loving Riels of Calidorn and that to none avail, ran mad in the forest."

Yea, even as Peire Vidal ran as a wolf for her of Penautier though some say that 'twas folly or as Garulf Bisclavret so ran truly, till the King brought him respite (See "Lais" of Marie de France), so was he ever by the Ash Tree.

Hear ye his speaking: (low, slowly he speaketh it, as one drawn apart, reflecting) (égaré).

---

* Referendum for contrast: "Daemonalitas" of the Rev. Father Sinistrari of Ameno (1600 circ). "A treatise wherein is shown that there are in existence on earth rational creatures besides man, endowed like him with a body and soul, that are born and die like him, redeemed by our Lord Jesus-Christ, and capable of receiving salvation or damnation." Latin and English text, pub. Liseux, Paris, 1879.

LA FRAISNE

(Scene: *The Ash Wood of Malvern*)

For I was a gaunt, grave councilor
   Being in all things wise, and very old,
   But I have put aside this folly and the cold
That old age weareth for a cloak.

I was quite strong—at least they said so—
The young men at the sword-play;
But I have put aside this folly, being gay
In another fashion that more suiteth me.

I have curled 'mid the boles of the ash wood,
I have hidden my face where the oak
Spread his leaves over me, and the yoke
Of the old ways of men have I cast aside.

By the still pool of Mar-nan-otha
Have I found me a bride
That was a dog-wood tree some syne.
She hath called me from mine old ways,
She hath hushed my rancour of council,
Bidding me praise

Naught but the wind that flutters in the leaves.

She hath drawn me from mine old ways,
Till men say that I am mad;
But I have seen the sorrow of men, and am glad,
For I know that the wailing and bitterness are a folly.
And I? I have put aside all folly and all grief.
I wrapped my tears in an ellum leaf
And left them under a stone
And now men call me mad because I have thrown
All folly from me, putting it aside

15

To leave the old barren ways of men,
Because my bride
Is a pool of the wood, and
Though all men say that I am mad
It is only that I am glad,
Very glad, for my bride hath toward me a great love
That is sweeter than the love of women
That plague and burn and drive one away.

Aie-e! 'Tis true that I am gay,
    Quite gay, for I have her alone here
    And no man troubleth us.

Once when I was among the young men . . .
And they said I was quite strong, among the young
        men.
Once there was a woman . . .
. . . but I forget . . . she was . . .
. . . I hope she will not come again.

. . . I do not remember. . . .

I think she hurt me once but . . .
That was very long ago.

I do not like to remember things any more.

I like one little band of winds that blow
In the ash trees here:
For we are quite alone
Here 'mid the ash trees.

CINO

Italian Campagna 1309, the open road

Bah! I have sung women in three cities,
    But it is all the same;
    And I will sing of the sun.

Lips, words, and you snare them,
Dreams, words, and they are as jewels,
Strange spells of old deity,
Ravens, nights, allurement:
And they are not;
Having become the souls of song.

Eyes, dreams, lips, and the night goes.
Being upon the road once more,
They are not.
Forgetful in their towers of our tuneing
Once for Wind-runeing
They dream us-toward and
Sighing, say, "Would Cino,
Passionate Cino, of the wrinkling eyes,
Gay Cino, of quick laughter,
Cino, of the dare, the jibe,
Frail Cino, strongest of his tribe
That tramp old ways beneath the sun-light,
Would Cino of the Luth were here!"

Once, twice, a year—
Vaguely thus word they:

"Cino?" "Oh, eh, Cino Polnesi
The singer is't you mean?"
"Ah yes, passed once our way,
A saucy fellow, but . . .
(Oh they are all one these vagabonds),
Peste! 'tis his own songs?
Or some other's that he sings?
But *you*, My Lord, how with your city?"

But you "My Lord," God's pity!
And all I knew were out, My Lord, you
Were Lack-land Cino, e'en as I am,
O Sinistro.

I have sung women in three cities.
But it is all one.
I will sing of the sun.
. . . eh? . . . they mostly had grey eyes,
But it is all one, I will sing of the sun.

   " 'Pollo Phoibee, old tin pan, you
     Glory to Zeus' aegis-day,
     Shield o' steel-blue, th' heaven o'er us
     Hath for boss thy lustre gay!

     'Pollo Phoibee, to our way-fare
     Make thy laugh our wander-lied;
     Bid thy 'fulgence bear away care.
     Cloud and rain-tears pass they fleet!

     Seeking e'er the new-laid rast-way
     To the gardens of the sun . . .
      . . . . . .

I have sung women in three cities
But it is all one.

I will sing of the white birds
In the blue waters of heaven,
The clouds that are spray to its sea.

IN EPITAPHIUM EIUS

SERVANT and singer, Troubador
That for his loving, loved each fair face more
Than craven sluggard can his life's one love,

Dowered with love, "whereby the sun doth move
And all the stars."
They called him fickle that the lambent flame
Caught "Bicé" dreaming in each new-blown name,

And loved all fairness though its hidden guise
Lurked various in half an hundred eyes;

That loved the essence though each casement bore
A different semblance than the one before.

NA AUDIART

Que be-m vols mal

Note: Anyone who has read anything of the troubadours knows well the tale of Bertrans of Born and My Lady Maent of Montaignac, and knows also the song he made when she would none of him, the song wherein he, seeking to find or make her equal, begs of each pre-eminent lady of Langue d'Oc some trait or some fair semblance: thus of Cembelins her "esgart amoros," to wit, her love-lit glance, of Aelis her speech free-running, of the Vicomtess of Chalais her throat and her two hands, at Roacoart of Anhes her hair golden as Iseult's; and even in this fashion of Lady Audiart "although she would that ill come unto him" he sought and praised the lineaments of the torse. And all this to make "Una dompna soiseubuda," a borrowed lady or, as the Italians translated it, "Una donna ideale."

THOUGH thou well dost wish me ill,
                    Audiart, Audiart,
     Where thy bodice laces start
As ivy fingers clutching through
Its crevices,
             Audiart, Audiart,
Stately, tall, and lovely tender
Who shall render
             Audiart, Audiart,
Praises meet unto thy fashion?
Here a word kiss!

          Pass I on
Unto Lady "Miels-de-Ben,"
Having praised thy girdle's scope,
How the stays ply back from it;
I breathe no hope
That thou shouldst . . .

                         Nay no whit
Bespeak thyself for anything.
Just a word in thy praise, girl,
Just for the swirl
Thy satins make upon the stair,
'Cause never a flaw was there
Where thy torse and limbs are met:
Though thou hate me, read it set
In rose and gold,*
Or when the minstrel, tale half told,
Shall burst to lilting at the praise:
                         Audiart, Audiart.

Bertrans, master of his lays,
Bertrans of Aultaforte thy praise
Sets forth, and though thou hate me well,
Yea though thou wish me ill,
                         Audiart, Audiart.
Thy loveliness is here writ till,
                         Audiart,
Oh, till thou come again.†
And being bent and wrinkled, in a form
That hath no perfect limning, when the warm
Youth dew is cold
Upon thy hands, and thy old soul
Scorning a new, wry'd casement,

Churlish at seemed misplacement,
Finds the earth as bitter
As now seems it sweet,
Being so young and fair
As then only in dreams,
Being then young and wry'd,
Broken of ancient pride,
Thou shalt then soften,
Knowing, I know not how,
Thou wert once she
                    Audiart, Audiart,
For whose fairness one forgave
                              Audiart,
Audiart,
        Que be-m vols mal.

VILLONAUD FOR THIS YULE

Towards the Noel that morte saison
   (Christ make the shepherds' homage dear!)
   Then when the grey wolves everychone
Drink of the winds their chill small-beer
And lap o' the snows food's gueredon
Then makyth my heart his yule-tide cheer
(Skoal! with the dregs if the clear be gone!)
Wineing the ghosts of yester-year.

Ask ye what ghost I dream upon?
(What of the magians' scented gear?)
The ghosts of dead loves everyone
That make the stark winds reek with fear
Lest love return with the foison sun
And slay the memories that me cheer
(Such as I drink to mine fashion)
Wineing the ghosts of yester-year.

Where are the joys my heart had won?
*(Saturn and Mars to Zeus drawn near!)**
Where are the lips mine lay upon,
Aye! where are the glances feat and clear
That bade my heart his valor don?

I skoal to the eyes as grey-blown meer
(Who knows whose was that paragon?)
Wineing the ghosts of yester-year.

* *Signum Nativitatis.*

Prince: ask me not what I have done
Nor what God hath that can me cheer
But ye ask first where the winds are gone
Wineing the ghosts of yester-year.

A VILLONAUD
BALLAD OF THE GIBBET

Or the Song of the Sixth Companion

(Scene: *"En ce bordeau ou tenons nostre estat"*)

It being remembered that there were six of us with Master Villon, when that expecting presently to be hanged he writ a ballad whereof ye know:

"Frères humains qui après nous vivez."

D RINK ye a skoal for the gallows tree!
François and Margot and thee and me,
Drink we the comrades merrily
That said us, "Till then" for the gallows tree!

Fat Pierre with the hook gauche-main,
Thomas Larron "Ear-the-less,"
Tybalde and that armouress
Who gave this poignard its premier stain,
Pinning the Guise that had been fain
To make him a mate of the "Hault Noblesse"
And bade her be out with ill address
As a fool that mocketh his drue's disdeign.

Drink we a skoal for the gallows tree!
François and Margot and thee and me,
Drink we to Marienne Ydole,
That hell brenn not her o'er cruelly.

Drink we the lusty robbers twain,
Black is the pitch o' their wedding dress,*
Lips shrunk back for the wind's caress
As lips shrink back when we feel the strain
Of love that loveth in hell's disdeign,
And sense the teeth through the lips that press
'Gainst our lips for the soul's distress
That striveth to ours across the pain.
Drink we skoal to the gallows tree!
François and Margot and thee and me,
For Jehan and Raoul de Vallerie
Whose frames have the night and its winds in fee.

Maturin, Guillaume, Jacques d'Allmain,
Culdou lacking a coat to bless
One lean moiety of his nakedness
That plundered St. Hubert back o' the fane:
Aie! the lean bare tree is widowed again
For Michault le Borgne that would confess
In "faith and troth" to a traitoress
"Which of his brothers had he slain?"

But drink we skoal to the gallows tree!
François and Margot and thee and me:

These that we loved shall God love less
And smite alway at their faibleness?

Skoal!! to the gallows! and then pray we:
God damn his hell out speedily
And bring their souls to his "Haulte Citee."

---

* Certain gibbeted corpses used to be coated with tar as a preservative;
thus one scarecrow served as warning for considerable time. See Hugo
L'Homme Qui Rit.

MESMERISM

"And a cat's in the water-butt"

Robert Browning, "Mesmerism"

Aye you're a man that! ye old mesmerizer,
    Tyin' your meanin' in seventy swadelin's,
    One must of needs be a hang'd early riser
To catch you at worm turning, Holy Odd's bodykins!

"Cat's i' the water butt!" Thought's in your verse-
    barrel,
Tell us this thing rather, then we'll believe you,
You, Master Bob Browning, spite your apparel
Jump to your sense and give praise as we'd lief do.

You wheeze as a head-cold long-tonsilled Calliope,
But God! what a sight you ha' got o' our innards,
Mad as a hatter but surely no Myope,
Broad as all ocean and leanin' man-kin'ards.

Heart that was big as the bowels of Vesuvius,
Words that were wing'd as her sparks in eruption,
Eagled and thundered as Jupiter Pluvius,
Sound in your wind past all signs o' corruption.

Here's to you, Old Hippety-hop o' the accents,
True to the Truth's sake and crafty dissector,
You grabbed at the gold sure; had no need to pack cents
Into your versicles.
                Clear sight's elector!

FIFINE ANSWERS

"Why is it that, disgraced, they seem to relish life the more?" "Fifine at the Fair," *VII*, 5.

SHARING his exile that hath borne the flame,
  Joining his freedom that hath drunk the shame
  And known the torture of the Skull-place hours,
Free and so bound, that mingled with the powers
Of air and sea and light his soul's far reach,
Yet strictured did the body-lips beseech
"To drink": "I thirst." And then the sponge of gall.

Wherefor we wastrels that the grey road's call
Doth master and make slaves, and yet make free,
Drink all of life and quaffing lustily
Take bitter with the sweet without complain
And sharers in his drink defy the pain
That makes you fearful to unfurl your souls.

We claim no glory. If the tempest rolls
About us we have fear, and then
Having so small a stake grow bold again.
We know not definitely even this
But cause some vague half-knowing half doth miss
Our consciousness and leaves us feeling
That somehow all is well, that sober, reeling
From the last carouse, or in what measure
Of so-called right or so-damned wrong our leisure
Runs out uncounted sand beneath the sun,
That, spite your carping, still the thing is done
With some deep sanction, that, we know not how,
Without our thought gives feeling; you allow
That 'tis not need we *know* our every thought

Or see the workshop where each mask is wrought
Wherefrom we view the world of box and pit,
Careless of wear, just so the mask shall fit
And serve our jape's turn for a night or two.

Call! eh bye! the little door at twelve!

I meet you there myself.

ANIMA SOLA

"Then neither is the bright orb of the sun greeted nor yet either the shaggy might of earth or sea, thus then, in the firm vessel of harmony is fixed God, a sphere, round, rejoicing in complete solitude."

Empedokles.

EXQUISITE loneliness:
　　Bound of mine own caprice,
　　I fly on the wings of an unknown chord
　That ye hear not,
　Can not discern.
My music is weird and untamèd,
Barbarous, wild, extreme,
I fly on the note that ye hear not,
On the chord that ye can not dream.
And lo, your out-worn harmonies are behind me
　　As ashes and mouldy bread,
I die in the tears of the morning,
　　I kiss the wail of the dead.
My joy is the wind of heaven,
　　My drink is the gall of night,
My love is the light of meteors;
　　The autumn leaves in flight.

I pendant sit in the vale of fate,
　　I twine the Maenad strands,
And lo, the three Eumenides
　　Take justice at my hands.
For I fly in the gale of an unknown chord.
The blood of light is God's delight
And I am the life blood's ward.

O Loneliness, O Loneliness,
Thou boon of the fires blown
From heaven to hell and back again,
Thou cup of the God-man's own!

For I am a weird untamèd
That eat of no man's meat,
My house is the rain ye wail against,
My drink is the wine of sleet.

My music is your disharmony
Intangible, most mad,
For the clang of a thousand cymbals
Where the sphinx smiles o'er the sand,
And viol strings that out-sing kings
Are the least of my command.
Exquisite, alone, untrammeled,
I kiss the nameless sign
And the laws of my inmost being
Chant to the nameless shrine.
I flee on the wing of a note ye know not,
My music disowns your law,
Ye can not tread the road I wed

And lo! I refuse your bidding.
I will not bow to the expectation that ye have.
Lo! I am gone as a red flame into the mist,
My chord is unresolved by your counter-harmonies.

IN TEMPORE SENECTUTIS

For we are old
    And the earth passion dieth;
        We have watched him die a thousand times,
When he wanes an old wind cryeth,
    For we are old
And passion hath died for us a thousand times
    But we grew never weary.

Memory faileth, as the lotus-loved chimes
    Sink into fluttering of wind,
    But we grow never weary
    For we are old.

The strange night-wonder of your eyes
Dies not, though passion flyeth
    Along the star fields of Arcturus
And is no more unto our hands;
    My lips are cold
And yet we twain are never weary,
And the strange night-wonder is upon us,
The leaves hold our wonder in their flutterings,
The wind fills our mouths with strange words
    For our wonder that grows not old.

The moth hour of our day is upon us
    Holding the dawn;
There is strange night-wonder in our eyes
Because the moth hour leadeth the dawn
As a maiden, holding her fingers,
The rosy, slender fingers of the dawn.

He: "Red spears bore the warrior dawn of old.
          Strange! Love, hast thou forgotten
             The red spears of the dawn,
             The pennants of the morning?"

She: "Nay, I remember, but now
          Cometh the dawn, and the moth hour
             Together with him; softly,
             For we are old."

FAMAM LIBROSQUE CANO

Your songs?
                Oh! The little mothers
        Will sing them in the twilight,
And when the night
Shrinketh the kiss of the dawn
That loves and kills,
What time the swallow fills
Her note, then the little rabbit folk
That some call children,
Such as are up and wide,
Will laugh your verses to each other,
Pulling on their shoes for the day's business,
Serious child business that the world
Laughs at, and grows stale;
Such is the tale
—Part of it—of thy song-life.

Mine?

        A book is known by them that read
        That same. Thy public in my screed
        Is listed. Well! Some score years hence
        Behold mine audience,
        As we had seen him yesterday.

        Scrawny, be-spectacled, out at heels,
Such an one as the world feels
A sort of curse against its guzzling
And its age-lasting wallow for red greed
And yet, full speed

Though it should run for its own getting,
Will turn aside to sneer at
'Cause he hath
No coin, no will to snatch the aftermath
Of Mammon.
Such an one as women draw away from
For the tobacco ashes scattered on his coat
And sith his throat
Shows razor's unfamiliarity
And three days' beard;

Such an one picking a ragged
Backless copy from the stall,
Too cheap for cataloguing,
Loquitur,

"Ah-eh! the strange rare name . . .
Ah-eh! He must be rare if even *I* have not . . ."
And lost mid-page
Such age
As his pardons the habit,
He analyzes form and thought to see
How I 'scaped immortality.

THE CRY OF THE EYES

Rest, Master, for we be aweary, weary
  And would feel the fingers of the wind
  Upon these lids that lie over us
Sodden and lead-heavy."

    Rest brother, for lo! the dawn is without!
The yellow flame paleth
And the wax runs low.

Free us, for without be goodly colors,
Green of the wood-moss and flower colors,
And coolness beneath the trees.

    Free us, for we perish
In this ever-flowing monotony
Of ugly print marks, black
Upon white parchment.

    Free us, for there is one
Whose smile more availeth
Than all the age-old knowledge of thy books:
And we would look thereon.

SCRIPTOR IGNOTUS

To K. R. H.

Ferrara 1715.

WHEN I see thee as some poor song-bird
 Battering its wings against this cage
  we call Today,
Then would I speak comfort unto thee,
From out the heights I dwell in, when
That great sense of power is upon me
And I see my greater soul-self bending
Sibylwise with that great forty-year epic
That you know of, yet unwrit
But as some child's toy 'tween my fingers,
And see the sculptors of new ages carve me thus,
And model with the music of my couplets
 in their hearts:
Surely if in the end the epic
And the small kind deed are one;
If, to God, the child's toy and the epic are the same.
E'en so, did one make a child's toy,
He might wright it well
And cunningly, that the child might
Keep it for his children's children
And all have joy thereof.

Dear, an' this dream come true,
Then shall all men say of thee,
"She 'twas that played him power at life's morn,
And at the twilight Evensong,
And God's peace dwelt in the mingled chords

She drew from out the shadows of the past,
And old-world melodies that else
He had known only in his dreams
Of Iseult and of Beatrice."

Dear, an' this dream come true,
I, who being poet only,
Can give thee poor words only,
Add this one poor other tribute,
This thing men call immortality.
A gift I give thee even as Ronsard gave it.
Seeing, before time, one sweet face grown old,·
And seeing the old eyes grow bright
From out the border of her fire-lit wrinkles,
As she should make boast unto her maids,
"Ronsard hath sung the beauty, *my* beauty,
          Of the days that I was fair."

So hath the boon been given, by the poets
        of old time,
(Dante to Beatrice—an' I profane not—)
Yet with my lesser power shall I not strive
          To give it thee?

All ends of things are with Him
From whom are all things in their essence.
If my power be lesser
Shall my striving be less keen?
But rather more! if I would reach the goal,
          Take then the striving!
"And if," for so the Florentine hath writ

When having put all his heart
Into his "Youth's Dear Book"
He yet strove to do more honor
To that lady dwelling in his inmost soul,
He would wax yet greater
To make her earthly glory more.
Though sight of hell and heaven were price thereof,
If so it be His will, with whom
Are all things and through whom
Are all things good,
Will I make for thee and for the beauty of thy music
A new thing
As hath not heretofore been writ.
    Take then my promise!

Note. Bertold Lomax, English Dante scholar and mystic, died in Ferrara in 1723, with his "great epic" still a mere shadow, a nebula crossed with some few gleams of wonder light. The lady of the poem was an organist of Ferrara, whose memory has come down to us only in Lomax's notes.

DONZELLA BEATA

Era mea
In qua terra
Dulce myrti floribus
  Rosa amoris
  Via erroris
Ad te coram veniam?

Soul,
  Caught in the rose-hued mesh
  Of o'er-fair earthly flesh,
Stooped you this thing to bear
Again for me? And be
Rare light to me, gold-white
In the shadowy path I tread?

Surely a bolder maid art thou
Than one in tearful, fearful longing
That should wait
Lily-cinctured at the gate
Of high heaven, star-diadem'd,
Crying that I should come to thee.

VANA

In vain have I striven
      to teach my heart to bow;
  In vain have I said to him,
"There be many singers greater than thou."

But his answer cometh, as winds and as lutany,
As a vague crying upon the night
That leaveth me no rest, saying ever,
          "Song, a song."

Their echoes play upon each other in the twilight
Seeking ever a song.
Lo, I am worn with travail
And the wandering of many roads hath made my eyes
As dark red circles filled with dust.
Yet there is a trembling upon me in the twilight,
    And little red elf words   crying "A song,"
    Little grey elf words   crying for a song,
    Little brown leaf words crying "A song,"
    Little green leaf words   crying for a song.
The words are as leaves, old brown leaves
    in the spring time,
Blowing they know not whither, seeking a song.

LI BEL CHASTEUS

THAT castle stands the highest in the land,
    Far-seen and mighty. Of the great hewn stones
    What shall I say? And deep foss way
That far beneath us bore of old
A swelling turbid sea
Hill-born and torrent-wise
Unto the fields below, where
Staunch villein and wandered
Burger held the land and tilled
Long laboring for gold of wheat grain
And to see the beards come forth
For barley's even tide.

But circle-arched, above the hum of life
We dwelt amid the ancient boulders,
Gods had hewn and druids runed
Unto that birth most wondrous, that had grown
A mighty fortress while the world had slept
And we awaited in the shadows there
While mighty hands had labored sightlessly
And shaped this wonder 'bove the ways of men.
Me seems we could not see the great green waves
Nor rocky shore by Tintagoel
From this our hold,
But came faint murmuring as undersong
E'en as the burgers' hum arose
And died as faint wind melody
Beneath our gates.

THAT PASS BETWEEN THE FALSE DAWN
AND THE TRUE

Blown of the winds whose goal is "No-man-knows"
   As feathered seeds upon the wind are borne,
   To kiss as winds kiss and to melt as snows
And in our passing taste of all men's scorn,
Wraiths of a dream that fragrant ever blows
From out the night we know not to the morn,
Borne upon winds whose goal is "No-man-knows."
An hour to each! We greet. The hour flows
And joins its hue to mighty hues out-worn
Weaving the Perfect Picture, while we torn
Give cry in harmony, and weep the Rose
Blown of the winds whose goal is "No-man-knows."

IN MORTE DE

O WINE-SWEET ghost, how are we borne apart
    Of winds that restless blow we know not where
    As little shadows smoke-wraith-sudden start
If music break the freighted dream of air;
So, fragile curledst thou in my dream-wracked heart,
So, sudden summoned dost thou leave it bare.
O wine-sweet ghost, how are we borne apart!
As little flames amid the dead coal dart
And lose themselves upon some hidden stair,
So futile elfin be we well aware.
Old cries I cry to thee as I depart,
"O wine-sweet ghost, how are we borne apart."

THRENOS

No more for us the little sighing,
  No more the winds at twilight trouble us.

Lo the fair dead!

No more do I burn.
No more for us the fluttering of wings
That whirred the air above us.

Lo the fair dead!

No more desire flayeth me,
No more for us the trembling
At the meeting of hands.

Lo the fair dead!

No more for us the wine of the lips,
No more for us the knowledge.

Lo the fair dead!

No more the torrent,
No more for us the meeting-place
(Lo the fair dead!)
Tintagoel.

COMRADERIE

"E tuttoque io fosse a la compagnia di molti, quanto alla vista."

SOMETIMES I feel thy cheek against my face
 Close-pressing, soft as is the South's first breath
 That all the subtle earth-things summoneth
To spring in wood-land and in meadow space.

Yea, sometimes in a bustling man-filled place
Me seemeth some-wise thy hair wandereth
Across my eyes, as mist that halloweth
The air a while and giveth all things grace.

Or on still evenings when the rain falls close
There comes a tremor in the drops, and fast
My pulses run, knowing thy thought hath passed
That beareth thee as doth the wind a rose.

BALLAD ROSALIND

Our Lord is set in his great oak throne
For our old Lord liveth all alone
    These ten years and gone.

A book on his knees and bent his head
For our old Lord's love is long since dead,
    These ten years and gone.

For our young Lord Hugh went to the East,
And fought for the cross and is crows' feast
    These ten years and gone.

"But where is our Lady Rosalind,
Fair as day and fleet as wind
    These ten years and gone?"

For our old Lord broodeth all alone,
Silent and grey in his black oak throne
    These ten years and gone.

Our old Lord broodeth silent there
For to question him none will dare
    These ten years and more.

Where is our Lady Rosalind
Fair as dawn and fleet as wind.
    These ten years and gone?

Our old Lord sits with never a word
And only the flame and the wind are heard
    These ten years and more.

. . .

"Father! I come," and she knelt at the throne,
"Father! know me, I am thine own.
    These ten years and more

"Have they kept me for ransom at Chastel d'Or
And never a word have I heard from thee
    These ten years and more."

But our old Lord answered never a word
And only sobbing and wind were heard.
    (These ten years and gone.)

We took our Lord and his great oak throne
And set them deep in a vault of stone
    These ten years and gone,

A book on his knees and bow'd his head
For the Lord of our old Lord's love is dead
    These ten years and gone,

And Lady Rosalind rules in his stead
(Thank we God for our daily bread)
    These ten years and more.

MALRIN

ALRIN, because of his jesting stood without, till all the guests were entered in unto the Lord's house. Then there came an angel unto him saying, "Malrin, why hast thou tarried?"

To whom, Malrin, "There is no feeding till the last sheep be gone into the fold. Wherefor I stayed chaffing the laggards and mayhap when it was easy helping the weak."

Saith the angel, "The Lord will be wroth with thee, Malrin, that thou art last."

"Nay, sirrah!" quipped Malrin, "I knew my Lord when thou and thy wings were yet in the egg."

Saith the angel, "Peace! Hasten lest there be no bread for thee, rattle-tongue."

"Ho," quoth Malrin, "is it thus that thou knowest my Lord? Aye! I am his fool and have felt his lash but me seems that thou hast set thy ignorance to my folly, saying, 'Hasten lest there be an end to his bread.'"

Whereat the angel went in in wrath. And Malrin, turning slowly, beheld the last blue of twilight and the sinking of the silver of the stars. And the suns sank down like cooling gold in their crucibles, and there was a murmuring amid the azure curtains and far clarions from the keep of heaven, as a muezzin crying, "Allah akbar, Allah il Allah! *It is finished.*"

And Malrin beheld the broidery of the stars become as wind-worn tapestries of ancient wars. And the memory of all old songs swept by him as an host blue-robèd trailing in dream, Odysseus, and Tristram, and the pale great gods of storm, the mailed Campeador and Roland and Villon's women and they of Valhalla; as a cascade of dull sapphires so poured they out of the mist and were gone. And above him the stronger clarion, as a muezzin crying, "Allah akbar, Allah il Allah! *It is finished.*"

And again Malrin, drunk as with the dew of old world druidings, was bowed in dream. And the third dream of Malrin was the dream of the seven, and no man knoweth it.

And a third time came the clarion and after it the Lord called softly unto Malrin, "Son, why hast thou tarried? Is it not fulfilled, thy dream and mine?"

And Malrin, "O Lord, I am thy fool and thy love hath been my scourge and my wonder, my wine and mine ecstasy. But one left me awroth and went in unto thy table. I tarried till his anger was blown out.

"Oh Lord, for the ending of a dream I kiss thee. For his anger is with the names of Deirdre and Ysolt. And our dream is ended, PADRE."

MASKS

These tales of old disguisings, are they not
    Strange myths of souls that found themselves
        among
Unwonted folk that spake an hostile tongue,
Some soul from all the rest who'd not forgot
The star-span acres of a former lot
Where boundless 'mid the clouds his course he swung,
Or carnate with his elder brothers sung
Ere ballad-makers lisped of Camelot?

Old singers half-forgetful of their tunes,
Old painters color-blind come back once more,
Old poets skill-less in the wind-heart runes,
Old wizards lacking in their wonder-lore:

All they that with strange sadness in their eyes
Ponder in silence o'er earth's queynt devyse?

ON HIS OWN FACE IN A GLASS

O STRANGE face there in the glass!
    O ribald company, O saintly host!
    O sorrow-swept my fool,

What answer?
            O ye myriad
That strive and play and pass,
Jest, challenge, counterlie,

I?   I?   I?

            And ye?

THE TREE

I STOOD still and was a tree amid the wood
  Knowing the truth of things unseen before,
  Of Daphne and the laurel bow
And that god-feasting couple olde
That grew elm-oak amid the wold.
'Twas not until the gods had been
Kindly entreated and been brought within
Unto the hearth of their heart's home
That they might do this wonder-thing.
Nathless I have been a tree amid the wood
And many new things understood
That were rank folly to my head before.

INVERN

EARTH's winter cometh
  And I being part of all
    And sith the spirit of all moveth in me
I must needs bear earth's winter.
Drawn cold and grey with hours
And joying in a momentary sun,
Lo I am withered with waiting till my spring cometh!
Or crouch covetous of warmth
O'er scant-logged ingle blaze,
Must take cramped joy in tomed Longinus
That, read I him first time
The woods agleam with summer
Or 'mid desirous winds of spring,
Had set me singing spheres
Or made heart to wander forth among warm roses
Or curl in grass nest 'neath a kindly moon.

PLOTINUS

As one that would draw through the node of things,
   Back-sweeping to the vortex of the cone,
   Cloistered about with memories, alone
In chaos, while the waiting silence sings:

Obliviate of cycles' wanderings
      I was an atom on creation's throne
      And knew all nothing my unconquered own.
God! Should I be the hand upon the strings?!

But I was lonely as a lonely child.
I cried amid the void and heard no cry,
And then for utter loneliness, made I
New thoughts as crescent images of *me*.
And with them was my essence reconciled
While fear went forth from mine eternity.

PROMETHEUS

For we be the beaten wands
    And the bearers of the flame.
    Our selves have died lang syne, and we
Go ever upward as the sparks of light
Enkindling all
'Gainst whom our shadows fall.

Weary to sink, yet ever upward borne,
Flame, flame that riseth ever
To the flame within the sun,
Tearing our casement ever,
For the way is one
That beareth upward
To the flame within the sun.

AEGUPTON

I—even I—am he who knoweth the roads
  Through the sky, and the wind thereof is my body.

I have beheld the Lady of Life,
I, even I, that fly with the swallows.

Green and grey is her raiment,
Trailing along the wind.

I—even I—am he who knoweth the roads
Through the sky, and the wind thereof is my body.

Manus animam pinxit—
My pen is in my hand

To write the acceptable word,
My mouth to chant the pure singing!

Who hath the mouth to receive it,
The song of the Lotus of Kumi?

I—even I—am he who knoweth the roads
Through the sky, and the wind thereof is my body.

I am flame that riseth in the sun,
I, even I, that fly with the swallows,

For the moon is upon my forehead,
The winds are under my kiss.

The moon is a great pearl in the waters of sapphire;
Cool to my fingers the flowing waters.

I—even I—am he who knoweth the roads
Of the sky, and the wind thereof is my body.

I will return unto the halls of the flowing
Of the truth of the children of Ashu.

I—even I—am he who knoweth the roads
Of the sky, and the wind thereof is my body.

BALLAD FOR GLOOM

FOR God, our God, is a gallant foe
    That playeth behind the veil.

I have loved my God as a child at heart
That seeketh deep bosoms for rest,
I have loved my God as maid to man
But lo, this thing is best:

To love your God as a gallant foe
       that plays behind the veil,
To meet your God as the night winds meet ·
       beyond Arcturus' pale.

I have played with God for a woman,
I have staked with my God for truth,
I have lost to my God as a man, clear-eyed,
    His dice be not of ruth,

For I am made as a naked blade,
    But hear ye this thing in sooth:

Who loseth to God as a man to man
    Shall win at the turn of the game.
I have drawn my blade where the lightnings meet
    But the ending is the same:
Who loseth to God as the sword blades lose
    Shall win at the end of the game.

For God, our God, is a gallant foe
       that playeth behind the veil;
Whom God deigns not to overthrow
    Hath need of triple mail.

FOR E. McC.

*That was my counter-blade
under Leonardo Terrone, Master of Fence*

Gone while your tastes were keen to you,
  Gone where the grey winds call to you,
    By that high fencer, even Death,
Struck of the blade that no man parrieth;
Such is your fence, one saith,
  One that hath known you.
Drew you your sword most gallantly,
Made you your pass most valiantly,
    'Gainst that grey fence, even Death.

Gone as a gust of breath.
Faith! no man tarrieth.
"*Se il cor ti manca*," but it failed thee not!
"*Non ti fidar*," it is the sword that speaks
"*In me.*"*

Thou trustedst in thyself and met the blade
'Thout mask or gauntlet, and art laid
As memorable broken blades that be
Kept as bold trophies of old pageantry,
As old Toledos past their days of war
Are kept mnemonic of the strokes they bore,

*Sword-rune: "If thy heart fail thee trust not in me."

So art thou with us, being good to keep
In our heart's sword-rack, though thy sword-arm sleep.

Envoi

Struck of the blade that no man parrieth
Pierced of the point that toucheth lastly all,
'Gainst that grey fencer, even Death,
Behold the shield! He shall not take thee all.

SALVE O PONTIFEX!

To Swinburne: an hemichaunt

ONE after one do they leave thee,
      High Priest of Iacchus,
        Toning thy melodies even as winds tone
The whisper of tree leaves, on sun-lit days.
Even as the sands are many
And the seas beyond the sands are one
In ultimate, so we here being many
Are unity. Nathless thy compeers,
      Knowing thy melody,
Lulled with the wine of thy music
Go seaward silently, leaving thee sentinel
O'er all the mysteries,
      High Priest of Iacchus.
For the lines of life lie under thy fingers,
And above the vari-colored strands
Thine eyes look out unto the infinitude
Of the blue waves of heaven,
And even as Triplex Sisterhood
Thou fingerest the threads knowing neither
Cause nor the ending.
      High Priest of Iacchus
Draw'st forth a multiplicity
Of strands, and beholding
The color thereof raisest thy voice
Toward the sunset,
      O High Priest of Iacchus!
And out of the secrets of the inmost mysteries
Thou chantest strange far-sourced canticles,
      O High Priest of Iacchus!

Life and the ways of Death, her
Twin-born sister, being Life's counterpart
(And evil being inversion of blessing
That blessing herself might have being)
And night and the winds of night;
Silent voices ministering to the souls
Of hermadryads that hold council concealèd
In streams and tree-shadowing
Forests on hill slopes,
   O High Priest of Iacchus,
All the manifold mystery
Thou makest wine of song of,
And maddest thy following
Even with visions of great deeds
And their futility, and the worship of love,
   O High Priest of Iacchus.
Wherefor though thy co-novices bent on the scythe
Of the magian wind that is voice of Prosephone,
Leaving thee solitary, master of initiating
Maenads that come through the
Vine-entangled ways of the forest
Seeking, out of all the world,
   Madness of Iacchus,
That being skilled in the secrets of the double cup
They might turn the dead of the world
Into beauteous paons,
   O High Priest of Iacchus,
Wreathed with the glory of years of creating
Entangled music that men may not
Over-readily understand:
     Breathe!

Now that evening cometh upon thee,
Breathe upon us that low-bowed and exultant
Drink, wine of Iacchus,
      That since the conquering*
Hath been chiefly contained in the numbers
Of them that even as thou have woven
Wicker baskets for grape clusters
Wherein is concealèd the source of the vintage,
      O High Priest of Iacchus,
Breathe thou upon us
    Thy magic in parting!
Even as they thy co-novices
Being mingled with the sea
While yet thou mad'st canticles
Serving upright before the altar
That is bound about with shadows
Of dead years wherein thy Iacchus
Looked not upon the hills, that being
Uncared for praised not him in entirety,
      O High Priest of Iacchus,
Being now near to the border of the sands
Where the sapphire girdle of the sea
      Encinctureth the maiden
Prosephone, released for the spring.
Look! Breathe upon us
The wonder of the thrice-encinctured mystery
Whereby thou being full of years art young
Loving even this lithe Prosephone
That is free for the seasons of plenty;

Whereby thou being young art old
And shalt stand before this Prosephone

* Vicisti, Nazarenus!

Whom thou lovest,
In darkness, even at that time
That she being returned to her husband
Shall be queen and a maiden no longer,

Wherein thou, being neither old nor young,
Standing on the verge of the sea
Shalt pass from being sand,
     O High Priest of Iacchus,
And becoming wave
     Shalt encircle all sands,
Being transmuted through all
The girdling of the sea.
     O High Priest of Iacchus,
Breathe thou upon us!

TO THE DAWN: DEFIANCE

Y E BLOOD-RED spears-men of the dawn's array
That drive my dusk-clad knights of dream away,
Hold! For I will not yield.

My moated soul shall dream in your despite
A refuge for the vanquished hosts of night
That *can* not yield.

THE DECADENCE

TARNISHED we! Tarnished! Wastrels all!
And yet the art goes on, goes on.
Broken our strength, yea as crushed reeds we
fall,
And yet the art, the *art* goes on.

Bearers of beauty flame and wane,
The sunset shadow and the rose's bloom.
The sapphire seas grow dull to shine again
As new day glistens in the old day's room.

Broken our manhood for the wrack and strain;
Drink of our hearts the sunset and the cry
"Io Triumphe!" Though our lips be slain
We see Art vivent, and exult to die.

REDIVIVUS

Hail Michael Agnolo! my soul lay slain
   Or else in torpor such, death seems more fair;
   I looked upon the light; if light were there
I knew it not. There seemed not any pain,
Nor joy, nor thought nor glorious deed nor strain
Of any song that half-remembered were
For sign of quickness in that soul; but bare
Gaunt walls alone me seemed it to remain.

Thou praisest Dante well, my Lord: "No tongue
Can tell of him what told of him should be
For on blind eyes his splendor shines too strong."
If so his soul goes on unceasingly
Shall mine own flame count flesh one life too long
To hold its light and bear ye company?

FISTULAE

"*To make her madrigal*
Who shall the rose sprays bring;
To make her madrigal
And bid my heart to sing?"

SONG

Love thou thy dream
  All base love scorning,
  Love thou the wind
And here take warning
That dreams alone can truly be,
For 'tis in dream I come to thee.

MOTIF

I HAVE heard a wee wind searching
    Through still forests for me,
    I have seen a wee wind searching
        O'er still sea.

Through woodlands dim
        Have I taken my way,
And o'er silent waters, night and day
Have I sought the wee wind.

Lady of rich allure,
  Queen of the spring's embrace,
    Your arms are long like boughs of ash,
Mid laugh-broken streams, spirit of rain unsure,
Breath of the poppy flower,
All the wood thy bower
    And the hills thy dwelling-place.

This will I no more dream;
Warm is thine arm's allure,
Warm is the gust of breath
That ere thy lips meet mine
Kisseth my cheek and saith:
"This is the joy of earth,
Here is the wine of mirth
    Drain ye one goblet sure,

Take ye the honey cup
The honied song raise up,
Drink of the spring's allure,
April and dew and rain;
Brown of the earth sing sure,
Cheeks and lips and hair
And soft breath that kisseth where
    Thy lips have come not yet to drink."

Moss and the mold of earth,
These be thy couch of mirth,
Long arms thy boughs of shade
April-alluring, as the blade
Of grass doth catch the dew
And make it crown to hold the sun.
Banner be you
        Above my head,
Glory to all wold display'd,
    April-alluring, glory-bold.

A ROUSE

SAVE ye, merry gentlemen! Vagabonds and rovers,
     Hell take the hin'most,
     We're for the clovers!
"Soul" sings the preacher.
     Our joy's the light.
"Goal" bawls ambition.
     Grass our delight!

Save ye, merry gentlemen!
     Whirr and dew of earth,
     Beauty 'thout raiment,
Reed pipes and mellow mirth
Scot free, no payment!

Gods be for heaven,
Clay the poet's birth!
     Save ye, merry gentlemen!
Wind and dew and spray o' sea,
     Hell take the hin'most,
Foot or sail for Arcady
Voice o' lark and breath of bee,
     Hell take the hin'most!
Our drink shall be the orange wine,
House o' boughs and roof o' vine,
     Hell take the hin'most!
Laugh and lips and gleam o' hair,
Fore-kiss breath, and shoulders bare,
     Save you queen o' April!

(La Regina Avrillouse loquitur.)

Follow! follow!

  Breath of mirth,
My bed, my bower green of earth,
  Naught else hath any worth.
Save ye, "jolif bachillier"!
  Hell take the hin'most!

NICOTINE

A Hymn to the Dope

Goddess of the murmuring courts,
  Nicotine, my Nicotine,
 Houri of the mystic sports,
  trailing-robed in gabardine,
Gliding where the breath hath glided,
Hidden sylph of filmy veils,
Truth behind the dream is veilèd
E'en as thou art, smiling ever, ever gliding,
Wraith of wraiths, dim lights dividing
Purple, grey, and shadow green,
  Goddess, Dream-grace, Nicotine.

Goddess of the shadow's lights,
  Nicotine, my Nicotine,
Some would set old Earth to rights,
  Thou and I none such I ween.
Veils of shade our dream dividing,
Houris dancing, intergliding,
Wraith of wraiths and dream of faces,
Silent guardian of the old unhallowed places,
Utter symbol of all old sweet druidings,
Mem'ry of witched wold and green,
  Nicotine, my Nicotine:

'Neath the shadows of thy weaving
Dreams that need no undeceiving,
Loves that longer hold me not,
Dreams I dream not any more,
Fragrance of old sweet forgotten places,
Smiles of dream-lit, flit-by faces,
All as perfume Arab-sweet
Deck the high road to thy feet

As were Godiva's coming fated
And all the April's blush belated
Were lain before her, carpeting
The stones of Coventry with spring,
So thou my mist-enwreathèd queen,
Nicotine, white Nicotine,
       Riding engloried in thy hair
Mak'st by-road of our dreams
         Thy thorough-fare.

IN TEMPORE SENECTUTIS

An anti-stave for Dowson

When I am old
      I will not have you look apart
      From me, into the cold,
Friend of my heart,
Nor be sad in your remembrance
Of the careless, mad-heart semblance
That the wind hath blown away
When I am old.

When I am old
And the white hot wonder-fire
Unto the world seem cold,
My soul's desire
Know you then that all life's shower,
The rain of the years, that hour
Shall make blow for us one flower,
Including all, when we are old.

When I am old,
If you remember
Any love save what is then
Hearth-light unto life's December,
Be your joy of past sweet chalices
To know then naught but this:
"How many wonders are less sweet
Than love I bear to thee
When I am old."

OLTRE LA TORRE: ROLANDO

THERE dwelt a lady in a tower high,
Foul beasts surrounded it,
I scattered them and left her free.

O-la! Oll-aa! The green-wood tree
Hath many a smooth sward under it!

My lady hath a long red cloak,
Her robe was of the sun,
This blade hath broke a baron's yoke,
That hath such guerdon won.

Yea, I have broke my Lord Gloom's yoke,
New yoke will I have none,
Save the yoke that shines in the golden bow
Betwixt the rain and the sun.

Ol-la! Ol-la! The good green-wood!
The good green-wood is free!
Say who will lie in the bracken high
And laugh, and laugh for the winds with me?

Make strong old dreams lest this our world lose heart.

For man is a skin full of wine
But his soul is a hole full of God
And the song of all time blows through him
As winds through a knot-holed board.

Though man be a skin full of wine
Yet his heart is a little child
That croucheth low beneath the wind
When the God-storm battereth wild.

A Quinzaine for This Yule

(1909)

A QUINZAINE FOR THIS YULE

Being selected from a
Venetian sketch-book
—" San Trovaso "—

———BY———
EZRA POUND

Title page of Pound's second book

To

The Aube of the West Dawn

BEAUTY should never be presented explained. It is Marvel and Wonder, and in art we should find first these doors—Marvel and Wonder—and, coming through them, a slow understanding (slow even though it be a succession of lightning understandings and perceptions) as of a figure in mist, that still and ever gives to each one his own right of believing, each after his own creed and fashion.

Always the desire to know and to understand more deeply must precede any reception of beauty. Without holy curiosity and awe none find her, and woe to that artist whose work wears its "heart on its sleeve."

WESTON ST. LLEWMYS
[E.P.]

PRELUDE

Over the Ognisanti

HIGH-DWELLING 'bove the people here,
  Being alone with beauty most the while,
  Lonely?
        How can I be,
Having mine own great thoughts for paladins
Against all gloom and woe and every bitterness?

Also have I the swallows and the sunset
And I see much life below me,
        In the garden, on the waters,
And hither float the shades of songs they sing
To sound of wrinkled mandolin, and plash of waters,
Which shades of song re-echoed
Within that somewhile barren hall, my heart,
Are found as I transcribe them following.

O Dieu, purifiez nos coeurs!
     Purifiez nos coeurs!

Yea, the lines hast thou laid unto me
     in pleasant places,
And the beauty of this thy Venice
     hast thou shown unto me
Until is its loveliness become unto me
     a thing of tears.

O God, what great kindness
     have we done in times past
     and forgotten it;
That thou givest this wonder unto us,
     O God of waters?

O God of the night
     what great sorrow
Cometh unto us,
     that thou thus repayest us
Before the time of its coming?

O God of silence,
     Purifiez nos coeurs,
     Purifiez nos coeurs,
For we have seen
The glory of the shadow of the
     likeness of thine handmaid,

Yea, the glory of the shadow
     of thy Beauty hath walked

Upon the shadow of the waters
    In this thy Venice.
        And before the holiness
Of the shadow of thy handmaid
    Have I hidden mine eyes,
      O God of waters.

O God of silence,
      Purifiez nos coeurs,
      Purifiez nos coeurs,
O God of waters,
      make clean our hearts within us
And our lips to show forth thy praise.
      For I have seen the
Shadow of this thy Venice
Floating upon the waters,
    And thy stars

Have seen this thing out of their far courses
Have they seen this thing,
      O God of waters.
Even as are thy stars
Silent unto us in their far-coursing,
Even so is mine heart
      become silent within me.

(Fainter)
      Purifiez nos coeurs
O God of the silence,
      Purifiez nos coeurs
O God of waters.

PURVEYORS GENERAL

PRAISE to the lonely ones!
  Give praise out of your ease
    To them whom the farther seas
Bore out from amongst you.

We, that through all the world
Have wandered seeking new things
And quaint tales, that your ease
May gather such dreams as please
    you, the home-stayers.

We, that through chaos have hurled
Our souls riven and burning,
Torn, mad, even as windy seas
Have we been, that your ease
Should keep bright amongst you:

That new tales and strange peoples
Such as the further seas
Wash on the shores of,
That new mysteries and increase
Of sunlight should be amongst you,
    you, the home-stayers.

Even for these things, driven from you,
Have we, drinking the utmost lees
Of all the world's wine and sorrowing,
Gone forth from out your ease,
          and borrowing
Out of all lands and realms
          of the infinite
New tales, new mysteries,
New songs from out the breeze
That maketh soft the far evenings,
Have brought back these things
          unto your ease,
Yours unto whom peace is given.

AUBE OF THE WEST DAWN:
VENETIAN JUNE

*From the tale "How Malrin chose for his Lady the
reflection of the Dawn and was thereafter true to her."*

WHEN svelte the dawn reflected in the west,
As did the sky slip off her robes of night,
I see to stand mine armouress confessed,
Then doth my spirit know himself aright,
And tremulous against her faint-flushed breast
Doth cast him quivering, her bondsman quite.

When I the dawn reflected in the west,
Fragile and maiden to my soul have pressed,
Pray I, her mating hallowed in God's sight,
That none asunder me with bale of might
From her whose lips have bade mine own be blest,
My bride, "the dawn reflected in the west."

I think from such perceptions as this arose the ancient myths
of the demi-gods; as from such as that in "The Tree" (*A Lume
Spento*), the myths of metamorphosis.

TO LA CONTESSA BIANZAFIOR

(CENT. XIV)

(Defense at Parting)

I

And all who read these lines shall love her then
    Whose laud is all their burthen, and whose
        praise
Is in my heart forever, though my lays
But stumble and grow startled dim again
When I would bid them, 'mid the courts of men,
Stand and take judgment. Whoso in new days
Shall read this script, or wander in the ways
My heart hath gone, shall praise her then.

Knowing this thing, "White Flower," I bid thy
        thought
Turn toward what thing a singer's love should be;
Stood I within thy gates and went not on,
One poor fool's love were all thy gueredon.
I go—my song upon the winds set free—
And lo!
        A thousand souls to thine are brought.

II

THIS fellow mak'th his might seem over
strong!"

Hath there a singer trod our dusty ways
And left not twice this hoard to weep her praise,
Whose name was made the glory of his song?

Hear ye, my peers! Judge ye, if I be wrong.
Hath Lesbia more love than all Catullus' days
Should've counted her of love? Tell me where strays
Her poet now, what ivory gates among?

Think ye? Ye think it not; my vaunt o'er bold?
Hath Deirdre, or Helen, or Beatrys,
More love than a maid unsung there is?

Be not these other hearts, when his is cold,
That seek thy soul with ardor manifold,
A better thing than were the husk of his?

III*

WHOSE is the gift of love? Tell me, whose is
⠀⠀⠀The right to give or take? The thing is mine?
⠀⠀⠀Think ye, O fools! It is not mine nor thine
Though I should strive, and I might strive y-wis,
Though I should strive what would we make o' this
Love for her soul, a love toward the divine,
A might within what heart that seeks such wine
As is the love betwixt her lips and his?

Were I to stand alone and guard this drink
To shut it off from such as come to pray,
What were the gueredon I bid ye think
To one that strove to hold the sun in goal?
Know ye first love, then come to me and say,
"Thou art inconstant and hast shamed thy soul."

[* This, and part IV on the next page, were omitted from the earlier printings of *A Quinzaine for This Yule*, perhaps because of space limitations. They were found in manuscript in the "San Trovaso" Notebook and are printed here for the first time, thus explaining—and eliminating—the cryptic "III" and "IV" that appeared below part II on page 14 of the original printing.]

IV

NIGHT and the wax wanes. Night, and the text
      grows dim.
        Who hath more love? Who brings more love?
  Speak strait.
Sung? Or unsung? Wedded? Or maid to wait
A thousand hearts who at the rune of him
That saw thy soul amid the Seraphim
Shall bear their incense to the horny gate
Whereby true dreams arise and hold their state?

Ye mock the lines. Pardon a poor fool's whim.

I, that have seen amid the dreams so much,
Speak dimly, stumble and draw forth your scorn.
Whether availeth more one prisoned man
Giving such labor as a bonds-man can,
Or a host of vagrants crying the morn
With "Hail" and "Day's grace" from the hearts o' such.

                ["queren lo jorn"]

PARTENZA DI VENEZIA

N<small>E'ER</small> felt I parting from a woman loved
   As feel I now my going forth from thee,
   Yea, all thy waters cry out "Stay with me!"
And laugh reflected flames up luringly.

O elf-tale land that I three months have known,
Venice of dreams, if where the storm-wrack drave
As some uncertain ghost upon the wave,
For cloud thou hidest and then fitfully
For light and half-light feign'st reality,
If first we fear the dim dread of the unknown
Then reassured for the calm clear tone:
"I am no spirit. Fear not me!"

As once the twelve storm-tossed on Galilee
Put off their fear yet came not nigh
Unto the holier mystery,
So we, bewildered, yet have trust in thee,
And thus thou, Venice,
                Show'st thy mastery.

LUCIFER CADITURUS

By SERVICE clomb I heaven
        And the law that smites the spheres,
        Turning their courses even,
Served me as I serve God.

And shall all fears
Of chaos or this hell the Mover dreams—
Because *he knows* what is to me yet dim—
Bid me to plod
An huckster of the sapphire beams
From star to star,
Giving to each his small embraced desire?
Shall I not bear this light
Unto what far
Unheavened bourne shall meet my fire
With some toward sympathy
That wills not rule?

By service clomb I heaven
And the Law served me, even
As I serve God; but shall this empery
Bid me restrict my course, or plod
A furrow worker in a space-set sod,
Or turn the emeralds of the empyrean
Because I dread some pale remorse
Should gnaw the sinews of m' effulgent soul
Deigned I to break His bonds
                That hold the law?

SANDALPHON

A<small>ND</small> these about me die,
    Because the pain of the infinite singing
    Slayeth them.
Ye that have sung of the pain of the earth-horde's
    age-long crusading,
Ye know somewhat the strain,
    the sad-sweet wonder-pain of such singing.
And therefore ye know after what fashion
This singing hath power destroying.

Yea, these about me, bearing such song in homage
Unto the Mover of Circles,
Die for the might of their praising,
And the autumn of their marcescent wings
Maketh ever new loam for my forest;
And these grey ash trees hold within them
All the secrets of whatso things
They dreamed before their praises,
And in this grove my flowers,
Fruit of prayerful powers,
Have first their thought of life
    And then their being.

Ye marvel that I die not! *forsitan!*
Thinking me kin with such as may not weep,
Thinking me part of them that die for praising
—Yea, though it be praising,
Past the power of man's mortality to
Dream or name its phases,

—Yea, though it chaunt and paean
Past the might of earth-dwelt
Soul to think on,
—Yea, though it be praising
As these the winged ones die of.

Ye think me one insensate
        else die I also
Sith these about me die,
And if I, watching
Ever the multiplex jewel, of beryl and jasper
   and sapphire,
Make of these prayers of earth ever new flowers;
Marvel and wonder!
Marvel and wonder even as I,
Giving to prayer new language
And causing the words to speak
Of the earth-horde's age-lasting longing,
Even as I marvel and wonder, and know not,
Yet keep my watch in the ash wood.

THE angel of prayer according to the Talmud stands unmoved
among the angels of wind and fire, who die as their one song is
finished; also, as he gathers the prayers they turn to flowers in his
hands.

Longfellow also treats of this, but as a legend rather than a
reality.

FORTUNATUS

RESISTLESS, unresisting, as some swift spear upon
        the flood
    Follow'th the river's course and tarries not
But hath the stream's might for its on-sped own,
So towards my triumph, and so reads the will,
'Gainst which I will not, or mine eyes grow dim,
And dim they seem not, nor are willed to be.
For beauty greet'th them through your London rain,
That were of Adriatic beauty loved and won,
And though I seek all exile, yet my heart
Doth find new friends and all strange lands
Love me and grow my kin, and bid me speed.

CAUGHT sometimes in the current of strange happiness borne upon
   such winds as Dante beheld whirling the passion-pale shapes in
the nethergloom,* so here in the inner sunlight, or above cool, dew-
green pasture lands, and again in caves of the azure magic.

WESTON ST. LLEWMYS
[E.P.]

      *E paion sì al vento esser leggieri.

      Ombre portate dalla detta briga.

BEDDOESQUE

——and going heavenward leaves
An opal spray to wake, a track that gleams
With new-old runes and magic of past time
Caught from the sea deep of the whole man-soul,
The "mantra" of our craft, then to the sun,
New-brought and broken by the fearless keel,
That were but part of all the sun-smit sea,
Have for a space their individual being,
And do seem as things apart from all Time's hoard,
The great whole liquid jewel of God's truth.

GREEK EPIGRAM

Day and night are never weary,
　　Nor yet is God of creating
　　　For day and night their torch-bearers
The aube and the crepuscule.

So, when I weary of praising the dawn and the sunset,
Let me be no more counted among the immortals;
But number me amid the wearying ones,
Let me be a man as the herd,
And as the slave that is given in barter.

CHRISTOPHORI COLUMBI TUMULUS

From the Latin of Hipolytus Capilupus,
early cent. MDC

Genoan, glory of Italy, Columbus thou sure light,
Alas! the urn takes even thee so soon out-blown.
Its little space

Doth hold thee, whom Oceanus had not the might
Within his folds to hold, although his broad embrace
Doth hold all lands.

Bark-borne beyond his bound'ries unto Hind thou wast
Where scarce Fame's volant self the way had cast.

THE AMPHORA

To T. H.

BRING me this day some poet of the past,
    Some unknown shape amid the wonder lords!
    Yea, of such wine as all time's store affords
From rich amphorae that nor years can blast
With might of theirs and blows down-rainèd fast,
Falernian and Massic of the Roman hoards,
I've drunk the best that any land accords,
Yet dread the time that I shall drink the last.

Bring me this day from out the smoky room
Some curved clay guardian of untasted wine
That holds the sun at heart. Search i' the gloom,
Boy, well, and mark you that the draught be good.
Then as an answer to this jest of mine,
Luck brought th' amphora, and the clasp was "HOOD."

HISTRION

No man hath dared to write this thing as yet,
   And yet I know, how that the souls of all men
      great
At times pass through us,
And we are melted into them, and are not
Save reflexions of their souls.
Thus am I Dante for a space and am
One François Villon, ballad-lord and thief,
Or am such holy ones I may not write
Lest blasphemy be writ against my name;
This for an instant and the flame is gone.

'Tis as in midmost us there glows a sphere
Translucent, molten gold, that is the "I"
And into this some form projects itself:
Christus, or John, or eke the Florentine;
And as the clear space is not if a form's
Imposed thereon,
So cease we from all being for the time,
And these, the Masters of the Soul, live on.

NEL BIANCHEGGIAR

BLUE-GREY, and white, and white-of-rose,
　　The flowers of the west's fore-dawn unclose.
　　I feel the dusky softness whirr
Of color, as upon a dulcimer
"Her" dreaming fingers lay between the tunes,
As when the living music swoons
But dies not quite, because for love of us
—Knowing our state
How that 'tis troublous—
It wills not die to leave us desolate.

With thanks to Marco Londonio for his delightful Italian para-
phrase of these lines appearing in *La Bauta* for August 9th [1908].

Some Poems from
the "San Trovaso" Notebook

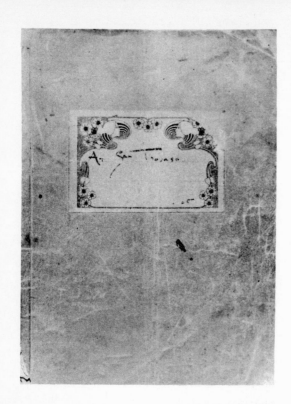

Cover of the "San Trovaso" sketch-book which was recently rediscovered

Manuscript of "Sonnet of the August Calm" from the "San Trovaso" sketch-book

THE "SAN TROVASO" NOTEBOOK

During the latter part of his stay in Venice in 1908, my
father lived at Calle dei Frati 942 in the San Trovaso
quarter of the city. The poems he wrote at that time are
preserved in holograph in a small copybook of the kind
which Italian schoolchildren still use for their exercises.
It bears the legend "At San Trovaso" on the cover label.
For the most part the poems appear to be fair copies
of the final versions, though there are some pages of
revisions and uncompleted drafts.

The importance of this period in his literary life
may be guessed from the way he has woven it into the
fabric of the *Cantos*. Briefly at first in Canto 3:

"I sat on the Dogana's steps
For the gondolas cost too much that year."

But years later in the *Pisan Cantos* he gives more detail
(Canto 76), including the time and place of the com-
position of these "San Trovaso" poems:

"well, my window
looked out on the Squero where Ogni Santi
meets San Trovaso
things have ends and beginnings."

He was not entirely confident about his first book *A
Lume Spento*, then in the process of being printed by A.
Antonini at Venice:

"shd/ I chuck the lot into the tide-water?
le bozze "A Lume Spento"/
and by the column of Todero
shd/ I shift to the other side."

Happily, he did not chuck the proofs into the canal, and
went on writing poems that summer. The words "shift
to the other side," apart from referring to his "contem-
plating a different way of life" (as he explained to me
recently), may be taken to mean "crossing the Grand
Canal." As the gondolas were expensive, he would walk
over the Ponte dell'Accademia—referred to in the *Pisan*

Cantos as "the new bridge of the Era"—and buy himself baked sweet potatoes at the corner cook-stall. His supper consisted mainly of a plate of *minestra d'orzo*, barley soup—"in my time/an orzo" (Canto 102).

What happened to the "San Trovaso" Notebook after his stay in Venice is difficult to follow. Some of the poems in it were published in the Christmas pamphlet *A Quinzaine for This Yule*, when he moved to London toward the end of 1908. After that, it seems to disappear until about ten years ago when I found it, in my grandfather's trunk, for Homer L. Pound was a conscientious collector of his son's papers. Not long afterward I asked my father's permission to publish some of the poems in it which seemed worth preserving. I received a very scathing answer. But his Italian publisher Vanni Scheiwiller persisted, and finally consent was given for "Statement of Being" and "For Italico Brass" to be included in the little volume dedicated to *A Lume Spento* which appeared in Scheiwiller's Pesce d'Oro series in commemoration of the fiftieth anniversary of Ezra Pound's first book and his seventy-third birthday.

Now the poet's attitude towards his earliest work is somewhat less severe, although his critical standards have not wavered—as can be judged from the foreword to this new edition. When recently I suggested that while this early work may not help "the young" technically, the feelings expressed in it might teach a lesson in this age of rage and cynicism, and that therefore it can be offered not merely as a "literary curiosity" but as further evidence of what stuff a young poet's dreams should be made of, he seemed satisfied.

> "Le Paradis n'est pas artificiel
> States of mind are inexplicable to us"

Brunnenburg, 1964   Mary de Rachewiltz

SAN VIO

OLD powers rise and do return to me
    Grace to thy bounty, O Venetian sun.
    Weary I came to thee, my romery
A cloth of day-strands raveled and ill-spun,
My soul a swimmer weary of the sea,
The shore a desert place with flowers none.

Old powers rise and do return to me.
The strife of waves, their lusty harmony
A thundered thorough bass the rocks upon,
Makes strong forgotten chanteys, and anon
My heart's loud-shouted burden proves to thee
Old powers risen have returned to me.

ROUNDEL FOR ARMS

ALL blood and body for the sun's delight,
   Such be the forms, that in my song bid spring,
   Should lead my lyric where the ways be dight
With flowers fit for any garlanding
And bid the lustre of our arms be bright
Who do our chaunting 'gainst the "Lord Gloom" fling.

All blood and body for the sun's delight,
I bid ye stand my words, and in the fight
Bear ye as men and let your glaive-strokes ring
Basnet on falchion 'till the chorusing
Proclaim your triumph and ye stand aright,
All blood and body for the sun's delight.

[Cino]

ROUNDEL
AFTER JOACHIM DU BELLAY

I COME unto thee through the hidden ways,
  Soul of my soul, whose beauty quivereth
  Within her eyes to whom my former days
As wined libation poured I, while my breath
Strove to her homage in unskillful lays
And bade my heart make his high vaunt 'gainst death.

I come unto thee through the hidden ways
Who art the soul of beauty, and whose praise
Or color, or light, or song championeth.
And of whom Time as but an herald saith,
"Trust though thou sense not, spite of my delays,
Her whom I bring thee through the hidden ways."

[Cino]

SONNET OF THE AUGUST CALM

WHEN summer hath her noon, it likes me lie
　　Somewhile quite parted from the stream of
　　　　things,
Watching alone the clouds' high wanderings,
As free as they are in some wind-free sky,

While naught but weirds of dream as clouds glide by
Or come as faint blown wind across the strings
Of this old lute of mine imaginings
And make it whisper me quaint runes and high.

In such a mood have I such strange sooth seen
And shapes of wonder and of beauty's realm
Such habitants, that times uncertainty
Upwells within me and doth nigh o'erwhelm
My body's life, until Truth dawns to me
That where the treasure is the heart hath been.

　　　　　　　　　　[San Trovaso]

TO YSOLT, FOR PARDON

My songs remade that I send greet the world
Thou knowest as at first they came to me,
Freighted with fragrance of thyself and furled
In stumbling words that yet us seemed to be
True music, sith thy heart and mine empurled
Their outer sense with inner subtlety.

My songs remade that I send greet the world
Me seem as red leaves of the autumn whirled
Out through the dust-grey ways, that dearer we,
As green bough-banners, had more lovingly
With simpler color than these turn-coats hurled,
As songs remade sent forth to greet the world.

MASTER Will, so cussed human,
Careless-clouted god o' speech,
Is there twist o' man or woman
Too well-hidden for thy reach?

Diadems and broken roses,
Wind and Tritons loud at horn,
Sack-stains half thy screed discloses,
The other half doth hold the morn.

————

SOME comfort 'tis to catch Will Shaxpeer stealing.
All bards are thieves save Villon, master thief,
Who pilfered naught but wine and then, wide
reeling,
Lilted his heart out,
Ballad-Lord in chief.

XCVIII

[AFTER SHAKESPEARE'S SONNET]

WHEN proud-pied April leadeth in his train
And yellow crocus quickneth to the breath
Of Zephyr fleeting from the sun-shot rain,
Then seek I her whom mine heart honoureth.
She is a woodland sprite and suzerain
Of every power that flouteth wintry death.

When proud-pied April leadeth in his train
And freeth all the earth from cold's mort-main,
Then with her fairness mine heart journeyeth
Through bourgeon wood-ways wherein tourneyeth
Earth's might of laughter 'gainst all laughter slain
Ere proud-pied April led in feat his train.

ALMA SOL VENEZIAE

Thou that hast given me back
　　Strength for the journey,
　　Thou that hast given me
　　Heart for the tourney,

O Sun venezian,
　　Thou that through all my veins
Hast bid the life-blood run,
Thou that hast called my soul
　　From out the far crevices,
Yea, the far dark crevices
　　And caves of ill-fearing,

　　　Alma tu sole!
Cold, ah a-cold
Was my soul in the caves of ill-fearing.

　　　　　　　　　　　[San Vio]

BALLAD OF WINE SKINS

As winds through a round smooth knot-hole
   Make tune to the time of the storm,
   The cry of the bard in the half-light
Is chaos bruised into form.

The skin of my wine is broken,
Is sunken and shrunken and old.
My might is the might of thistle down,
My name as a jest out-told.

Yet there cometh one in the half-light
That shieldeth a man with her hair,
And what man crouch from in his soul
The child of his heart shall bear.

Bibliographical Note

A Lume Spento, Ezra Pound's first book, appeared in June 1908. It was printed in Venice by A. Antonini in an edition of 100 copies. The book has never since been reprinted, though some of the poems appeared in Pound's later books, such as *Personae*. (A small book of the same title, issued by Vanni Scheiwiller in Milan in 1958 to celebrate the fiftieth anniversary of Pound's first publication, included only seven of the original poems.)

A Quinzaine for This Yule was first published in London in the middle of December 1908 by Pollock & Co., and later in the same month, with a few corrections, by Elkin Mathews. Each printing was of 100 copies. Only a few of the poems were reprinted in later Pound collections.

For fuller accounts, see *A Bibliography of Ezra Pound* by Donald Gallup (London, 1963).

Index of Titles and First Lines